Do-It-Yourself Science™

EXPERIMENTS
on
ROCKS
and the
ROCK CYCLE

Zella Williams

PowerKiDS press.

New York

Published in 2007 by The Rosen Publishing Group, Inc.
29 East 21st Street, New York, NY 10010

First Edition

Editor: Joanne Randolph
Book Design: Greg Tucker and Ginny Chu
Photo Researcher: Sam Cha

Photo Credits: Cover image copyright Jim Lopes, 2006. Used under license from Shutterstock, Inc.; p. 5 © Royalty-Free/Corbis; pp. 6, 7, 8, 9, 10, 11, 12, 13, 14, 15, 18, 19, 20, 21 by Cindy Reiman; pp. 16, 17 by Adriana Skura.

Library of Congress Cataloging-in-Publication Data

Williams, Zella.
  Experiments on rocks and the rock cycle / Zella Williams. — 1st ed.
     p. cm. — (Do-it-yourself science)
  Includes bibliographical references and index.
  ISBN-13: 978-1-4042-3660-8 (lib. bdg.)
  ISBN-10: 1-4042-3660-0 (lib. bdg.)
  1. Rocks—Experiments—Juvenile literature. 2. Geology—Experiments—Juvenile literature. I. Title.
  QE432.2.W487 2007
  552.0078—dc22
                                        2006024880

Manufactured in the United States of America

Contents

Rocks and the Rock Cycle 4

Hot Spots and Igneous Rock 6

Glaciers Shape Earth................................8

Erosion in Action....................................10

An Igneous Rock Is Born...........................12

Make a Metamorphic Rock.........................14

Making Crystals 16

It's Sedimentary!...................................18

Hunting for Fossils 20

What Did You Learn?..............................22

Glossary 23

Index 24

Web Sites..24

Rocks and the Rock Cycle

Rocks can be found everywhere on Earth. In fact, the whole top **layer**, or surface, of Earth is made of rock. This layer is called the crust, and it makes up the ground we walk on and the ocean floor.

There are three kinds of rock that make up Earth's crust. These are igneous rocks, sedimentary rocks, and metamorphic rocks. Each kind of rock can change into either of the other kinds of rock. The way these rocks change is called the rock cycle.

This rock has been shaped by weathering and erosion, two steps in the rock cycle.

Hot Spots and Igneous Rock

Earth's crust floats on a layer of hot, melted rock. Sometimes this melted rock rises up through a hole in Earth's crust. It **erupts** onto the surface as **lava**. The place where this happens is called a volcano. The lava from a volcano cools and hardens into igneous rock. Let's see how a special kind of volcano called a hot spot works.

You will need

- an 8½-by-11-inch (22 x 28 cm) piece of poster board
- a pair of scissors, a tool with two sharp blades used for cutting
- a large tube of toothpaste
- a friend

1

Carefully poke a line of small holes about 1 inch (2.5 cm) apart in a piece of poster board. Each hole should fit the tip of your smallest finger. The holes are like the small openings in Earth's crust.

2

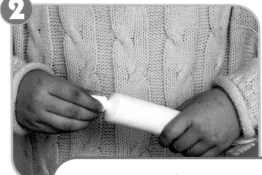

Open a tube of toothpaste and hold it so that the opening is pointing up. The toothpaste stands for the melted rock that rises from under Earth's crust.

3

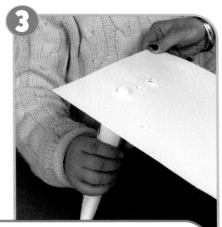

Have a friend hold the poster board over the tube of toothpaste so that the first hole lines up with the opening of the tube. The poster board is like a moving plate of Earth's crust. Carefully press the tube.

4

Slowly move the poster board over each hole. Press the tube so that a little bit of toothpaste comes out of each hole as the board moves by. As the crust moves over a hot spot, the melted rock rises onto Earth's surface and cools to make igneous rock. This is how hot spots form a row of islands or mountains.

Glaciers Shape Earth

Glaciers play a part in Earth's rock cycle. Glaciers are large pieces of ice that move very slowly. As a glacier moves, it picks up pieces of rock and **sediment**. It carries these bits of rock and sediment along and then leaves them behind somewhere else. You can see how glaciers shape Earth in this **experiment**.

You will need

- 1 cup (237 ml) of honey
- ½ cup (118 g) of sprinkles
- a dinner plate
- a pile of paper cloths
- 1 tablespoon (15 ml) of water

1

Rest one-half of a dinner plate on a pile of paper cloths. You want one side of the plate to be higher than the other, like a hill.

2

Sprinkle a small handful of the sprinkles in a line across the center of the plate. If the sprinkles slide off, try getting the plate a little wet and then put on the sprinkles.

3

Carefully put 1 tablespoon (15 ml) of honey onto the higher side of the plate, covering some of the sprinkles. What happens? The honey may move slightly downhill, but not much. This very small movement is like what happens when a small amount of ice gathers in one place on Earth.

4

Add the rest of the honey to the honey already on the plate. This time the honey moves down the plate and pushes some of the sprinkles along as it goes. As a glacier grows, it does the same thing on Earth. It slowly pushes rocks and sediment down a hill.

Erosion in Action

Many forces keep the rock cycle moving. Erosion is one of them. Erosion is the wearing down and carrying away of rock over time. Wind, ice, rain, and moving water can erode rock. Over time the small bits of eroded rock become sedimentary rock. Try this to see how moving water causes erosion.

You will need

- 3 clear glasses
- 3 pieces of coated candy, like Skittles or M&M's
- 2 cups (473 ml) of water
- tape
- a felt-tip pen
- a piece of paper
- a pair of scissors
- a timer

1 Write a 1, 2, and 3 on a piece of paper. Cut each number out and tape one to each glass. Fill glasses 1 and 2 with 1 cup (237 ml) of water. Leave glass 3 empty.

2 Drop a piece of candy into each glass.

3 Pick up glass 1 and shake it carefully for about 1 minute. By moving the water around the candy, you cause the water to erode the candy. Do this once every 10 minutes for 1 hour. Leave the other two glasses alone.

4 Look at the candy in each glass. The piece in glass 1 **dissolved** much more than the pieces in glasses 2 and 3 because of the erosion you created. The still water in glass 2 caused some, but not much, of the candy to dissolve. The candy in glass 3 looks the same because the air did not erode it.

An Igneous Rock Is Born

Igneous rocks are formed when a **mixture** of hot, melted rock cools and hardens. This melted mixture inside Earth is called magma. When magma reaches Earth's surface, often through volcanoes, it is called lava. By using food found in the kitchen, you can make something that will help show how igneous rocks form.

You will need

- 1 can of evaporated milk
- 2 cups (448 g) of sugar
- 12 ounces (340 g) of chocolate chips
- a large dish
- waxed paper to line the dish
- a pot
- a stove

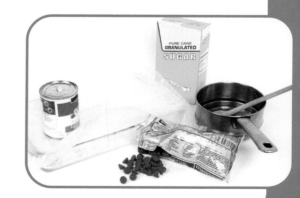

1

In a pot heat a can of evaporated milk until it is warm. Add the sugar and mix until it dissolves. Then slowly add the chocolate chips and stir until they melt and mix with the milk and sugar. This mixture is like the melted rock that makes up magma and lava.

2

Pour the mixture into a dish lined with waxed paper. The mixture spreads in the dish just like lava spreads over Earth.

3

Put the mixture in the refrigerator overnight. In the morning the liquid will have cooled and hardened. This is like what happens to real magma and lava as they cool and harden into igneous rock.

Make a Metamorphic Rock

Rocks that are heated and then **squeezed** deep inside Earth are called metamorphic rocks. An igneous rock, a sedimentary rock, or even a metamorphic rock can be heated and squeezed to become a new metamorphic rock. You can follow some of the steps that go into making a metamorphic rock right in your kitchen.

You will need

- blue clay that can be baked
- yellow clay that can be baked
- a 1-foot (30.5 cm) piece of string
- a cookie sheet
- an oven

1

Have an adult help you preheat the oven to the heat shown on the box your clay comes in.

2

Think of each color of clay as a different type of **mineral**. Rocks are made up of minerals. Push and mix your minerals together to make a ball. Pushing the clay together is like the squeezing that happens to rocks deep inside Earth.

3

Take one end of the string in each hand and pull your hands apart until the string is tight. Use the string to cut the ball of clay in half. This gives you a better view of the inside of your "metamorphic rock."

4

Place the two pieces of clay on a cookie sheet and bake them as directed on the box. The oven's heat is like the heat from deep inside Earth. Take the cookie sheet out and let it cool. The clay should have hardened like a metamorphic rock would.

Making Crystals

All rocks are made of two or more minerals. When minerals form slowly, they take on a shape called a crystal. Crystals have a fixed and orderly form. They often have flat sides. You have likely seen some crystals, such as salt crystals and sugar crystals. You can make crystals by doing this experiment.

You will need

- black construction paper
- a pie pan
- a measuring cup
- a tablespoon
- Epsom salt
- warm water
- scissors
- a spoon

1 Cut a piece of black construction paper to fit the bottom of a pie pan.

2 Dump 1 tablespoon (14 g) of Epsom salt into ¼ cup (59 ml) of warm water. Stir until the salt dissolves.

3 Dump this mixture onto the construction paper in the pie pan. Put the pan near a sunny window. When the Epsom salt and water mixture dries, you can see tiny crystals on the black paper.

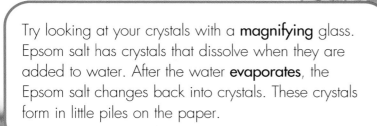

4 Try looking at your crystals with a **magnifying** glass. Epsom salt has crystals that dissolve when they are added to water. After the water **evaporates**, the Epsom salt changes back into crystals. These crystals form in little piles on the paper.

It's Sedimentary!

A sediment is a tiny mineral or a bit of rock that has eroded from a larger rock. Wind and water pick up and move sediments to new places. Over time more sediments settle on top of the old sediments. The new layers press on the lower layers. The sediments are pushed together and harden. They become sedimentary rock. You can start your own sedimentary rock.

You will need

- three colors of sand
- salt
- an 8-ounce (24 cl) glass

1

Pour about ½ inch (13 mm) of sand in the bottom of the glass. Sand is made of quartz, a clear, hard mineral, and other minerals. This is your first layer of minerals.

2

Now add a layer of salt, which is another mineral. Keep doing steps 1 and 2 until you have many layers of minerals.

3

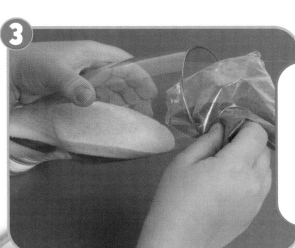

If the layers were pressed together with a lot of weight for a long time, they would harden into sedimentary rock. Layers of sand aren't always flat. Empty your glass and make some new layers. This time try tipping the glass after each layer and see what happens.

Hunting for Fossils

Fossils are often found in sedimentary rock. Are there fossils hiding in your neighborhood? Take a look! Be sure to write down what you see or draw a picture. Then try to find out more. Ask questions. What living thing formed the fossil? When and how did it form? Start hunting.

You will need

- a pad of paper
- a pencil
- a magnifying glass

1 Take a walk through your neighborhood. Ask an adult to go with you because some fossils are hard to find.

2 If you see a sidewalk, look closely at it. Do you see any places where people or animals walked on the sidewalk before it was dry? These are **modern** fossils. Write and draw what you see in your notebook.

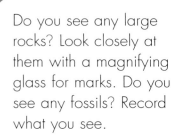

3 Do you see any large rocks? Look closely at them with a magnifying glass for marks. Do you see any fossils? Record what you see.

4 Look for animal tracks, marks left by leaves on the ground, and other marks. If left alone, these marks could someday form fossils. Record what you find in your notebook.

What Did You Learn?

What have you learned about rocks and the rock cycle? You have found out a little bit about the three kinds of rock found on Earth. You have also found out some of the things that help form these rocks. Earth and the rocks on Earth are always changing.

Take a look at some rocks and see what you can find out about them. Doing these experiments was your first step to becoming a rock **detective**.

Glossary

detective (dih-TEK-tiv) A person who finds facts and solves crimes.

dissolved (dih-ZOLVD) Broke down.

erupts (ih-RUPTS) Breaks open.

evaporates (ih-VA-puh-rayts) Changes from a liquid, like water, to a gas, like steam.

experiment (ek-SPER-uh-ment) A set of steps done on something to learn more about it.

fossils (FAH-sulz) The hardened remains of a dead animal or plant.

lava (LAH-vuh) Hot, melted rock that erupts from a volcano.

layer (LAY-er) One thickness of something.

magnifying (MAG-nuh-fy-ing) Making something appear larger than it is.

mineral (MIN-rul) Something in nature that is not an animal, a plant, or another living thing.

mixture (MIKS-cher) A new thing that is made when two or more things are mixed together.

modern (MO-dern) Having to do with today or using the most up-to-date ideas or ways of doing things.

sediment (SEH-deh-ment) Bits of rock, sand, or mud carried by wind or water.

squeezed (SKWEEZD) Forced together.

Index

C
crust, 4, 6–7

E
Earth, 4, 8–9, 12–15, 22
experiment(s), 8, 16, 22

F
fossil(s), 20–21

G
glacier(s), 8–9
glass(es), 11, 19
ground, 4, 21

I
ice, 8–10
igneous rock(s), 4, 6–7, 12, 14

L
lava, 6, 12–13
layer(s), 4, 6, 18–19

M
magnifying glass, 17, 21
metamorphic rock(s), 4, 14–15
mineral(s), 15–16, 18–19
mixture, 12–13, 17

P
plate, 7, 9
poster board, 7

S
sedimentary rock(s), 4, 10, 14, 18–20
sediment(s), 8–9, 18
surface, 4, 6–7

V
volcano(es), 6, 12

W
water, 10–11, 17–18

Web Sites

Due to the changing nature of Internet links, PowerKids Press has developed an online list of Web sites related to the subject of this book. This site is updated regularly. Please use this link to access the list:

www.powerkidslinks.com/diysci/rocks/